## SCUPS

This sticky-footed monster can stick to almost any surface should the need arise. Its feet use air to produce a call that travels vast distances. Scups like Quibbles and harpsitrees.
**THEY CANNOT LIVE ON THE PLANT, EARTH OR COLD ISLANDS.**

## NOGGIN

This rock-like creature brings a steady beat to the islands it inhabits by beating its giant hands on its head. Noggins like Drumplers and trumplites.
**THEY CANNOT LIVE ON THE COLD ISLAND.**

## POMPOM

This perfect-pink cheerleader gets its colour from eating only red food. The PomPom dances and emits a boisterous cry to be noticed. PomPoms like Fwogs and bottomless pits.
**THEY CANNOT LIVE ON THE PLANT, COLD OR WATER ISLANDS.**

## POTBELLY

This single-element plant monster has two heads that bleat intermittently. Its sound is a welcome addition to the chorus but can be a troublemaker. Potbellies like T-Roxes and eerie remains.
**THEY CANNOT LIVE ON THE AIR ISLAND.**

## TWEEDLE

This bird-like monster loves to be sociable, flying around from monster to monster spreading secrets and gossip. Tweedles like Cybops and reflecting pools.
**THEY CANNOT LIVE ON THE PLANT ISLAND.**

On each spread you need to find a Breeding Structure, a Nursery and a Unity Tree.

# LEAFY LAND

Welcome to **PLANT ISLAND**. This was once a sleepy, serene place, but now the monsters are here, a cheerful song fills the air!

Can you find:

PANGO

CONGLE

FLOOFY NEST

MELDABLEND

WILD BAGPIPE

# PINK PARTY

There's a **POMPOM** party on **AiR ISLAND**. They are only serving red food and no Potbellies are allowed. **YiPPEE YaY!**

Can you find:

CYBOP

RiFF

BARBLOO STATUE

FiRE BUSH

9

# WATER WORLD

This tranquil isle has awoken with a splash! The vibrant coral is a perfect back drop for a monster symphony.

Can you find:

PUMMEL

SPUNGE

REFLECTING POOL

SQUEED STATUE

TOOB

# Lava Land

**EARTH ISLAND** is bubbling with magma and music! The monsters here really rock out, all accompanied by the great harmonising **QUARRISTER**.

**Can you find:**

DRUMPLER

SHRUBB

BEEYOOT TREE

HARPSITREE

PIPES OF CICADO

13

# MYSTERIOUS MELODIES

**ETHEREAL ISLAND** is an otherworldly dimension full of strange creatures. The sublime wonder of their song is hard to resist!

**Can you find:**

WHiSP

SOX

YUMYUM TREE

TREE FORT TOWER

15

THE FURCORN has landed on PLANT ISLAND and he has brought his family of melody-makers! These precious green monsters can certainly belt out a tune!

# FROZEN FIESTA

Cold winds are blowing but the monsters are still having a good time! The Wubbox have started a dance-off accompanied by the sounds of the chorus.

# Scups Spectacular

The Scups love Water Island. They have overtaken this puddle-prone place to make funky music with their sticky feet.

**Can you find:**

3 x SPUNGE EGGS

2 x DANDIDOO

DRAGON TOWER

# ZUFFLe RiOT

Earth Island has turned into a forest of Zuffle trees. The fiesty monsters of this unpredictable zone are concealed amongst the Zuffles' fluffy leaves.